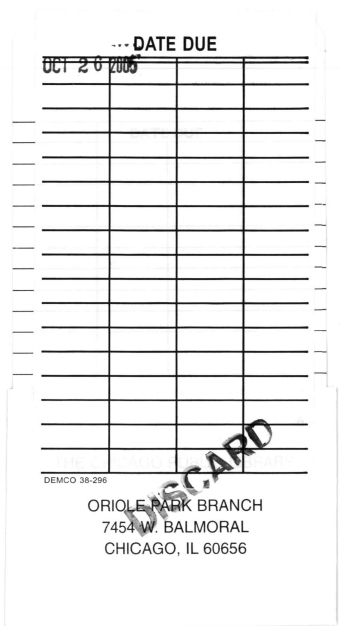

Science Experiments

SOLIDS, LIQUIDS, AND GASES

by
John Farndon

BENCHMARK BOOKS

MARSHALL CAVENDISH
NEW YORK

Marshall Cavendish Corporation

99 White Plains Road

Tarrytown, New York 10591

© Marshall Cavendish Corporation, 2002

Created by Brown Partworks Ltd

Library of Congress Cataloging-in-Publication Data

Farndon, John.

    Solids, liquids, and gases / by John Farndon.

        p. cm. – (Science experiments)

Includes index.

ISBN 0-7614-1338-3

1.   Matter—Properties—Experiments—Juvenile literature. [1. Matter—
Properties—Experiments. 2. Experiments.] I. Title.

QC173.36.F37 2001

530.4—dc21   00-068017

Printed in Hong Kong

PHOTOGRAPHIC CREDITS

t – top; b – bottom; c – center; l – left; r – right

Corbis: title page, Jim McDonald (c); p5, David Spears (tr);
p10,11 Manuel Sanchis Calvete (b); p11, Jeremy Horner (tr); p15, Jean
Yves Ruszneiwksi (tr); p18,19 Jim McDonald (b); p21, Darrell Gulin (br);
p24,25 Darrell Gulin (b); p25, Martin Rogers (tr); p28, Jim McDonald (r)

Sylvia Cordaiy Photo Library Ltd: p4,5 (b)

Pictor International: p6, (b); p22, (bl)

The Image Bank: p14,15 Patrick J. LaCroix (b)

Leslie Garland Picture Library: p29, (tr)

Step-by-step photography throughout: Martin Norris

Front cover: Martin Norris

Contents

ALL ABOUT MATTER

Just about all of the Universe is empty space—but not all of it. Scattered throughout the Universe are tiny bits of stuff called matter.

Matter is every substance in the Universe—everything that is not empty space, from the tiniest speck of dust to the most gigantic star. Matter is what we are made of and what the world

and everything else in the Universe is made of.

Although there is a huge variety of matter, nearly all of it comes in just three basic forms—solid, liquid, and gas. Solids are hard like rock. You can see them and maybe even pick them up. Liquids are like water. They are harder to see and harder still to pick up

In this chilly Arctic scene, water exists as a solid (in ice), as liquid (in the sea), and as gas (as water vapor in the air).

without a container. Gases are like air, and often invisible and impossible to pick up.

Every kind of matter can come in these three forms, which scientists call the *states* (or *phases*) of matter. Each kind of matter can change from one state to another, just as ice turns to water when it gets warm, and water turns to steam when it gets hot. An iron bar may melt to a liquid when it gets hot. A drink may freeze solid when it gets cold. It all depends on how hot or cold it is.

In focus

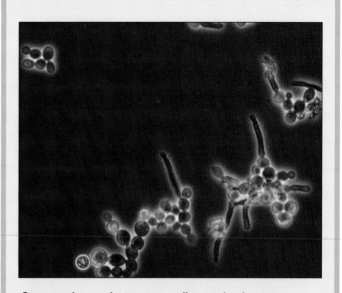

Seen under a microscope, pollen grains in water appear to move by themselves. In fact, they are knocked about by tiny, fast-moving water molecules.

MOVING ATOMS

This book may look solid but, like all the matter in the Universe, it's really empty space dotted with incredibly tiny, bits or particles, such as atoms and molecules. Atoms are so small you can see them only with special microscopes. You could fit two billion on the period at the end of this sentence. Atoms join together to make molecules, which are usually only a little bigger.

All kinds of matter, whether solid or liquid or gas, are made from atoms and molecules. These particles are constantly moving very fast. What makes solids, liquids, and gases different is the *way* the particles move. This is called the "kinetic" theory of matter. Kinetic comes from the Greek for "moving."

Particles are so small, and move so fast, that it is impossible to see them moving. But, in 1827, Scottish botanist Robert Brown looked at pollen grains floating in water and saw them moving about. We now know they move because they are being knocked by invisibly small water molecules. This is called Brownian motion.

SOLIDS

Solids are things such as rocks, brick walls, rubber balls, the metal in cars, the bones in your body, and much more. What all solids have in common is that they can be made into particular shapes. Once made into a shape, a solid tends to stay the same shape and size unless forced into a new shape. If a factory makes a brick, for instance, it will usually stay brick shaped.

Some solids, like concrete blocks, are really hard, and it takes a lot of force to change their shape. Other solids, like modeling clay and butter, are soft, and it is quite easy to change their shape.

Bridges are built from solids, like stone, because solids are rigid and keep their shape.

Did you know?

Diamonds are the world's hardest natural solids. They are so tough that saws with pieces of diamond in their blades can be used to cut through slabs of stone or even solid metal!

In focus

SOLID PARTICLES

Solids keep their shape because the particles they are made of are knitted tightly together. Just like magnetism pulls magnets together, so strong forces between the particles in a solid pull them together and hold them in place. They can vibrate in place, but they cannot move around.

In fact, most solids are "crystalline" (see page 10). This means the particles are knitted together in a pattern, called a lattice, that makes up tiny grains, or crystals. Solids such as glass and plastic, however, are noncrystalline, or "amorphous." In these, the particles are knitted together in a disorderly way. These solids are smooth rather than grainy.

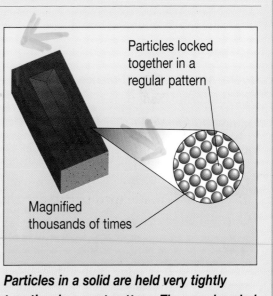

Particles locked together in a regular pattern

Magnified thousands of times

Particles in a solid are held very tightly together in a neat pattern. They are bonded together so firmly that they cannot move, but simply vibrate in place.

\# 2 All hard solids are difficult to reshape, but some can be broken quite easily—snapping like a twig, or shattering when hit, like china. Such solids are said to be brittle. Brittle solids are almost impossible to reshape; they will break instead of changing shape. But hard solids, such as many metals, are said to be "malleable." This means they can be hammered or beaten into new shapes. The word malleable comes from *malleus,* the Ancient Roman word for hammer.

Some solids, like nylon rope, are soft but difficult to tear apart. Solids like these are said to have great "tensile strength."

Although solids have a particular size and shape most of the time, this is not always the case. Some solids, like tar and chocolate, will bulge into different shapes on warm days without actually melting.

All solids—hard or soft, brittle or malleable—will stay solid only as long as they stay cool enough. As soon as they are warmed above a certain temperature, called the *melting point,* they will melt and become liquid. Each substance has its own melting point. Butter, tar, and chocolate will begin to melt even on a mildly warm day. But the heat of a furnace is needed to melt steel.

MELTING MOMENTS

You will need

- ✔ Several small heatproof dishes plus one large heatproof dish
- ✔ A candy thermometer
- ✔ Samples for testing, such as chocolate, butter, and gelatin
- ✔ A measuring cup
- ✔ A knife

Break the samples into small chunks, either by hand or with a knife. Put the chunks in the small heatproof dishes.

In the real world

MELTING POINT

Every substance is solid up to a certain temperature, after which, it melts to a liquid. Once liquid, it freezes (turns solid again) if the temperature drops back past the same point. So the melting point and freezing point are the same temperature. These are some typical melting points:

- Oxygen: –426°F (–219°C)
- Water: 32°F (0°C)
- Lead: 622°F (328°C)
- Iron: 2,802°F (1,539°C)
- Tungsten: 6,170°F (3,410°C)
- Diamond: 6,332°F (3,500°C)

Gently lower two of the sample dishes into the water, taking care the water does not spill into the dishes.

What is happening?

When a solid substance like gelatin is heated, its particles vibrate faster and faster. Eventually they are vibrating so vigorously that they break the bonds that hold them in place. So the substance melts and becomes a liquid. If it cools again, the particles will vibrate slower and slower until the bonds form one again. This is what happens when a substance freezes.

2 Put the large heatproof dish or pan on the stove and pour in water to fill it to a depth of an inch (2 cm) or so.

Ask an adult to turn on the burner at a low heat and to supervise the remainder of the experiment. Do not attempt to do this by yourself. Insert the candy thermometer in the water and keep checking the temperature as it slowly heats up. Watch the samples in the dishes and note the temperature of the water when each sample begins to melt. Keep checking, and note the temperature at which each sample is totally melted. When the samples have melted, turn the heat off and wait for the water to cool down. When it is quite cold, take out the dishes and repeat the experiment with the other samples.

CRYSTALS

If you look closely at the grains of sugar in a sugar bowl, you will see that they are tiny cubes. These cubes are called sugar crystals. Salt is made of crystals as well, though they are usually much smaller than sugar crystals. Gems such as diamonds and emeralds are crystals too.

In fact, most solids, including metals and rocks, are made up of crystals. You cannot always see the crystals in metal, because they are very small or firmly stuck together. But you can often see them in pieces of rock, if you use a magnifying glass.

Crystals are bits of solids that form in regular, geometrical shapes, with smooth faces and sharp edges. They come in chunks rather than rounded shapes. Many crystals are shiny or clear. They got their name from the glassy chunks of quartz crystal that the Greeks called *krystallos*. They thought it was a special kind of ice that would not melt.

In rock cavities, quartz can grow into large crystals. Pure quartz is clear, but traces of iron turn it to purple amethyst.

Did you know?

In 1880, French scientist Pierre Curie found that some crystals give a small electric current when squeezed. Also, a small electric current applied to these crystals makes them vibrate. This effect is called piezoelectricity. If pressure is applied to quartz crystals, for instance, an electric current or even a spark may be generated. This is how the lighters for gas stoves work. In a quartz watch, which contains a tiny quartz crystal, an electrical current from the watch's battery sets the crystal vibrating at exactly 32,678 times a second. The vibrations keep the watch's electric motor timed so exactly that quartz watches are accurate to within 60 seconds in a year.

Crystals in rocks don't always have a definite shape because they are packed too tightly. But if allowed to form freely in rock cavities, they grow into beautiful regular shapes. Scientists know that crystals get their regular shapes because they are made of atoms linked together in a neat structure, or "lattice."

Perfect crystals only form occasionally. Through careful study, scientists have realized that all crystals build up in one

In the real world

LIQUID CRYSTALS

Most crystals are solid, but when some special crystals warm up, they don't melt immediately. Instead, they go dark and turn semiliquid. These are called liquid crystals. When they warm up a

Liquid crystals are used for all portable computer screens.

little, they flow like a liquid, but their molecules keep some of their neat pattern, so they can hold their shape. The LCDs (liquid crystal displays) you see on portable computer screens and watches have clear liquid crystals held between two sheets of glass. To make the displays, small electrical currents are used to warm the crystals and make them go dark in exactly the right pattern.

of six basic shapes or "systems," such as in cubes, flat plates, or hexagonal rods. Each system reflects the crystal's lattice of atoms. By shining X rays through the crystal, scientists can analyze the lattice structure. This is called X-ray crystallography. Scientists used X-ray crystallography in the 1950s to discover the structure of DNA, the basic chemical in every cell that carries all of the instructions for life.

GROWING CRYSTALS

You will need

- Copper sulfate powder (from a pharmacist or science teacher)
- A jar, a pitcher, and a shallow dish
- Cotton thread
- A ruler or pencil
- Stirring stick

Beware!

Copper sulfate is poisonous and should only be handled under adult supervision.

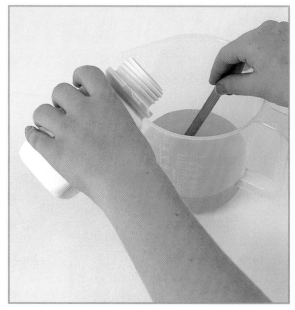

1 Stir copper sulfate powder into water until all the powder is dissolved. Add more powder until no more will dissolve.

In the real world

GIANT CRYSTALS

All crystals—and so most solids—develop by growing in a liquid containing the right molecules. Just how big they grow depends on the conditions. The biggest crystals grow in cavities deep underground. Here liquids heated by volcanic activity cool down very slowly, and, as they cool, substances dissolved within them crystallize. Even under these conditions, most single crystals are rarely bigger than a fist, and most are smaller. Occasionally, though, single crystals of the mineral beryl can grow as big as telephone poles.

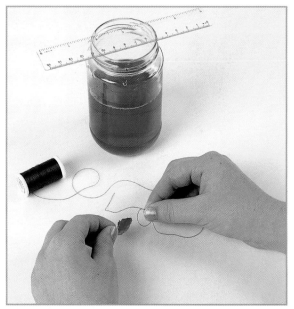

3 After a few days, take the biggest crystal from the dish (right) and tie a piece of thread around it. Fill a jar with the liquid.

2 Pour a little of the blue liquid (copper sulfate solution) into a shallow dish, then leave it to stand for a few days.

What is happening?

Adding the copper sulfate powder to the water creates a copper sulfate *solution*, which is copper sulfate dissolved in water. When you leave the solution to stand, the copper sulfate molecules are scattered throughout the water. But those molecules that are close to each other draw together and form a lattice. In this way, tiny crystals slowly begin to form. These crystals act like magnets and attract other molecules. The new arrivals add to the lattice and the crystal slowly grows. If one crystal is much bigger than all the others, it will draw all the spare molecules toward itself and grow bigger still.

Tie the free end of the thread to a ruler and suspend the crystal from it in the solution in the jar. Leave the jar in a dry, safe place. After about a week, you will find that the crystal from the dish has grown much bigger in the jar (right). Take out the crystal and gently wipe it dry on a kitchen towel. You now have a beautiful blue crystal. But be careful: it is very fragile and will dissolve instantly if you get it wet.

LIQUIDS

The most common liquid by far is water. But soft drinks, oil, wine, and milk are all liquids. Unlike solids, liquids cannot hold their shape. In fact, they flow into the shape of any container they are poured into.

All liquids flow, but some flow more easily than others. Oil flows slower than water, and thick paint flows slower still. A liquid's resistance to flow—its stickiness—is called its viscosity.

Although liquids flow into any shape, unlike gases, liquids always have a definite surface. Whenever

Milk is a special kind of liquid called a suspension. Solid fat particles are suspended within it.

In focus

When a solid melts and becomes a liquid, many of the bonds holding the molecules together break, so clusters of them wander in all directions. This is why liquids flow into any shape. Particles in a solid are like ranks of soldiers marching on the spot. Those in a liquid are more like dancers on a crowded dancefloor.

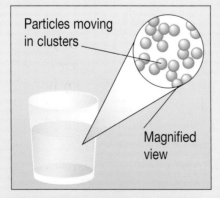

Particles moving in clusters

Magnified view

Clusters of molecules in a liquid such as water wander freely in all directions.

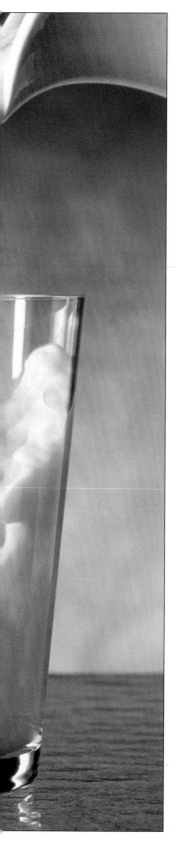

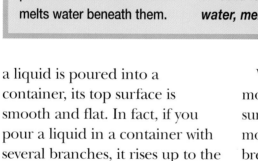

a liquid is poured into a container, its top surface is smooth and flat. In fact, if you pour a liquid in a container with several branches, it rises up to the same level in each branch.

Actually, the surface of a liquid is not always quite flat. If you look closely at the top of a glass filled to the brim with water, you will notice that the surface of the water curves up over the edge at the top of the glass. This bowing, called a meniscus, is due to an effect called surface tension. It is caused by the molecules in a liquid pulling together. When a bit of water falls through the air, it is surface tension that pulls the water into round drops.

When a liquid is heated, some molecules break free of the surface as the heat makes them move faster. The molecules that break free form a gas. Some form bubbles within the liquid, but most drift away from the liquid's surface. This is called evaporation. Once the liquid reaches the boiling point, it won't get any hotter; it just evaporates. Steam is tiny drops of evaporated water in the air. If the gas that has evaporated from a liquid cools down, it turns back into a liquid, often forming little droplets on cold surfaces. This is called condensation. Dew is water condensed from the air in the cool of the night.

LIQUID POWER

You will need

- A large plastic bowl
- Length of plastic tubing to fit on syringe
- Two syringes (such as for icing cakes)
- Waterproof tape (to seal joints)

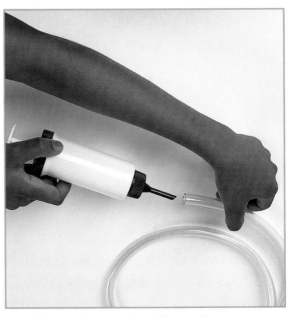

1 Screw the nozzle of the syringes on as tightly as you can, then insert one of them into the end of the plastic tube.

In the real world

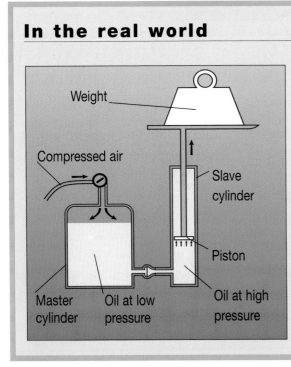

Weight

Compressed air

Slave cylinder

Piston

Master cylinder

Oil at low pressure

Oil at high pressure

HYDRAULIC POWER

Hydraulic machines use liquids such as oil to transmit power as in this experiment. They have a "master" cylinder, like the syringe you push in, and a "slave," like the one pushed out. They gain immense power by transferring a liquid from a larger, master, cylinder to a smaller slave. In this diagram of a hydraulic lift, the large piston is actually compressed air. This pushes a large volume of oil in the master into the narrower, slave cylinder. The effort applied to the master is hugely concentrated and multiplied in the slave, forcing out the piston and lifting the load that it is carrying.

Make sure the plunger of the other syringe is pushed in, then insert its nozzle, under water, into the other end of the tube. Now lift both plungers and the tube out of the water. Press in the plunger that is out, and you should see the other plunger move out.

2 Immerse the tube and syringe in a bowl of water, and pull out the plunger to draw water in.

What is happening?

Liquids may flow very easily, but, unlike gas, they cannot be squashed into a smaller space. In a gas, the particles are far apart and can be squeezed closer together. But in a liquid, although the particles are only loosely linked, they are so close together that they cannot be squeezed any closer—it is impossible to squeeze a liquid very much. Liquids are said to be incompressible. So, in this experiment, when you push one plunger in, the water must move down the tube because it cannot be squeezed. As the water moves down the tube, it pushes the other plunger out the other end.

GASES

Gases can be difficult to detect. The air all around you is made of gases, yet you cannot see them because they are transparent. You cannot feel gases either—except how warm or cold they are. You cannot pick them up or hold them. In fact, gases have no shape at all. They simply spread out to fill the whole container, no matter what size it is.

Indeed, the only way you would even be aware of many gases is from their smell. Some gases have a strong smell, like hydrogen sulfide, which smells like rotten eggs. But some gases, like the natural gas used for cooking and heating,

Gases spread out to fill any space—like the air you blow into a balloon. You can't see the air, but, as the balloon expands, you can tell that it is filling up with more air.

Did you know?

Gas particles move very quickly. This why you can smell a perfume almost the instant someone enters a room—the scent particles spread rapidly among the air particles and a few of them reach your nose. This process, in which gas particles mix with each other, is called diffusion.

do not even smell much. This is why gas companies often add another gas with an odor to the gas supply so that people can smell a gas leak.

Although gases are hard to pin down, they are matter, just like solids and liquids. Each gas has its own characteristics. Gases are very light and thin, but even the lightest gas, hydrogen, can be weighed. Some gases have their own color, such as nitrogen dioxide, which is brown.

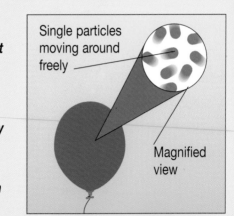

GASES AND VOLUME

You will need

- ✔ Baking soda
- ✔ White vinegar
- ✔ A small glass bottle
- ✔ A balloon
- ✔ A tablespoon
- ✔ A funnel

1 Use the funnel to fill the balloon with baking soda. Then pour ½ inch (1.2 cm) of vinegar into the bottle.

In focus

GAS LAW

Gases exert a push, or "pressure," on the things they meet. This is created by the combined impact of all the gas's moving particles. The more particles there are, the greater the pressure. Irish scientist Robert Boyle (1627–1691) showed that when you squeeze a gas, the pressure goes up in proportion, as long as the temperature stays the same. This is because you are squeezing more particles into a smaller space. If you heat up a gas but keep it in exactly the same sized container, its pressure goes up because the particles move faster. This is Boyle's Law.

2 Keeping the balloon hanging down, stretch its neck over the neck of the bottle as far as it will go.

What is happening?

Mixing baking soda with an acid like vinegar starts a vigorous chemical reaction that releases carbon dioxide. The gas takes up much more space than the solid and the liquid, so it inflates the balloon.

As soon as the balloon is securely stretched over the bottle, quickly lift it upright. Shake the balloon so that the soda drops straight down into the vinegar below. As soon as the soda meets the vinegar, it will start to fizz and froth rapidly and the balloon will inflate.

In the real world

WATER IN THE AIR

Like a wet sponge, the air is full of water. You can't see it, though, because water in the air is in the form of an invisible gas called water vapor. It forms as water evaporates from oceans and lakes. Air with water vapor in it is called humid. As humid air gets warmer, it expands and can hold more water, because there are bigger spaces between particles. When humid air cools, the spaces between the particles become smaller so the air cannot take in any more vapor. It is said to be saturated. The temperature at which this happens is called dew point. If it gets cooler still, the vapor will condense to form dew, fog or clouds.

Dew is drops of water that condense out of the warm air when the temperature drops to the dew point.

CHANGING PHASES

You will need

- ✔ Two plastic ice trays (for making ice in a freezer)
- ✔ Table salt
- ✔ A pitcher of water
- ✔ A spoon

1 Stir table salt into the pitcher of water. At first, it will all dissolve. Keep on adding salt until no more will dissolve.

Did you know?

Even on a warm day, you can shiver as you come out of water, because, as it dries off your skin, it draws away heat from your body.

Heating a substance does not always simply raise its temperature. When a solid melts or a liquid evaporates, just that little extra heat is needed to break the bonds between particles. Scientists call this extra heat latent heat. When a solid is at melting point, heat does not raise its temperature. Instead, it provides the latent heat needed to break the bonds between particles. As the bonds break, the solid melts. Similarly, when a liquid evaporates, it takes away extra heat from its surroundings. This is why sweating helps keep you cool. Sweat is warm water that evaporates from your skin. As sweat evaporates, it draws heat from your skin and so cools you.

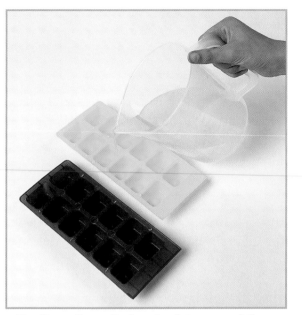

Every substance turns from liquid to solid as it gets colder. The temperature at which it turns solid is called the freezing point. Water normally freezes and turns to ice at 32°F (0°C). Adding salt lowers its freezing point by several degrees. Similarly, salt water in the ocean has a lower freezing point than fresh water in lakes and rivers. This is why the ocean does not normally freeze in winter. It only freezes over near the very cold North and South poles.

2 Pour the salted water into one of the ice trays. Fill the other tray with plain water. Place both trays in the freezer.

After about five hours, take the ice trays from the freezer. Closely examine them. You will find the tray of plain water has turned entirely to solid ice. The salt water in the other tray will be only partially frozen, or not frozen at all—unless your freezer is set to a very low temperature.

MIXTURES AND SOLUTIONS

Some substances are made of just one pure chemical, like pure gold and pure water. But most, such as milk, oil, the air, and most foods, are mixtures of different chemicals. The various chemicals in a mixture may be thoroughly mixed up, but they do not ever interact.

Like different marbles in a box, their molecules remain intact, and it is often possible to separate them from each other.

Water from the tap usually looks clear and pure. But even the cleanest tap water is actually a mixture, with traces of various other substances. In fact, tap

Seawater is a solution. Only about 96.5 percent is actually water. The rest is dissolved chemicals, mainly salts such as sodium chloride.

Did you know?

The blood that flows through your body is made of millions of tiny blood cells in a liquid, called plasma, but it is not the same as gas plasma (see page 29). Blood plasma is a solution, with many different substances, including proteins, dissolved in water.

water is a very particular kind of mixture called a solution.

In a solution, a solid, liquid, or gas (the solute) is dissolved in a liquid (the solvent). The molecules of the solute mingle so well with the molecules of the liquid that the solid vanishes. When you make instant coffee by pouring hot water on coffee powder, you are making a solution. The powder is the solute and the water the solvent.

As you dissolve more of the solute in a solvent, the solution becomes stronger and more concentrated. Eventually,

though, it will become saturated and no more will dissolve. You can, however, make a saturated solution absorb more by heating it. Heating expands the solution, increasing the space between its molecules and making more room for the solute to dissolve.

If a saturated solution is cooled or left to evaporate, it actually becomes more than saturated. Then the solute molecules may begin to link up so that crystals grow.

FINDING THE SOLUTION

You will need

✔ Tea bags
✔ A mug
✔ A deep saucer
✔ Sugar cubes
✔ Granulated sugar
✔ A teaspoon

1 Fill up a mug with warm water, adding the last few drops carefully so that the water bulges but does not overflow.

Now try this

Solubility tells us how much of a substance will dissolve in a liquid. The warmer a solution is, the more you can dissolve in it. You can prove this by counting how many lumps of sugar you can stir into a cup of cold tea before no more will dissolve. Now count how many lumps you can stir into a lukewarm cup of tea. Finally, count how many you can add to a cup of hot tea. More lumps will dissolve in the hot tea than in the cold tea. This is because solubility increases with the temperature.

Test the effect of temperature on solubility with cups of tea and some sugar lumps.

What is happening?

The particles in a liquid are not packed as tightly together as they are in a solid: there is actually a bit of space between them, and solids can dissolve into these spaces. When you add sugar to what seems like a full mug, it does not overflow, because the sugar slips into the spaces between the water particles. In warm water, there are bigger spaces between the particles than in cold water. This is why you can dissolve quite a bit of sugar in it. Only when all the spaces are full, will the water finally spill over the top of the mug.

2 Very, very carefully, pour a spoonful of sugar into the water and wait for the sugar to dissolve.

Go on adding more sugar bit by bit, waiting for it to dissolve each time. You will probably find you can add three or four more spoonfuls of sugar before the mug finally overflows.

THE FOURTH STATE

Whenever you see a bolt of lightning flash through the air, you are seeing gases being ionized. The massive heat and electrical surge is enough to ionize the surrounding air instantly.

On Earth, nearly all matter exists either as a solid, a liquid, or a gas. But, out in space, all of these are quite rare. In fact, 99 percent of all matter in the Universe exists in a fourth state, called a plasma, which is found very rarely here on Earth.

A plasma is formed when a gas is heated up to an extremely high temperature or shot through with a powerful electrical current. The effect of the heat or electricity is to strip tiny particles called electrons off some of the gas's atoms. This loss of electrons makes them electrically charged, so plasmas buzz with electricity.

Electrically charged atoms are called ions, so plasmas are often called ionized gases. As a plasma gets hotter or the electrical current gets stronger, more atoms become "ionized."

On Earth, the huge electrical charge of a lightning bolt ionizes the air, making it glow. So do even small electrical sparks. In fact, wherever you see a brilliant, cold electrical flash, the air is being turned into a plasma.

Out in space, the Sun and every star in the Universe are turned into plasmas by the immense heat of the nuclear reactions going on inside them. The Sun is so hot that streams of plasma radiate throughout the Solar System. This is known as solar wind.

In the real world

USING PLASMAS

The bright lights of a city are glowing plasmas, heated inside glass tubes by electrical currents.

Plasmas have all kinds of practical uses. Neon lights are a type of glowing plasmas. An electrical current is zapped through the gas inside the glass neon tube, turning it into a plasma. The different colors are produced by different gases. In carmaking, the electrical charge of plasmas is used to bond metals in electric arc welding. Certain flat computer screens use plasmas too. Some space rockets have even used plasma fuels for the long trips to Mars.

Scientists hope to use plasmas to generate electricity one day, by controlling "nuclear fusion," the same process that goes on inside stars. The heat generated from this process can reach 212,000,000°F (100,000,000°C), and would melt any container. But, as in a star, the reaction could instead be contained inside a plasma.

Experiments in Science

Science is about knowledge: it is concerned with knowing and trying to understand the world around us. The word comes from the Latin word, *scire*, to know.

In the early 17th century, the great English thinker, Francis Bacon, suggested that the best way to learn about the world was not simply to think about it, but to go out and look for yourself—to make observations and try out things. Ever since then, scientists have tried to approach their work with a mixture of observation and experiment. Scientists insist that an idea or theory must be tested by observation and experiment before it is widely accepted.

All the experiments in this book have been tried before, and the theories behind them are widely accepted. But that is no reason why you should accept them. Once you have done all the experiments in this book, you will know that the ideas are true not because we have told you that they are but because you have seen for yourself.

All too often in science, there is an external factor interfering with the result that the scientist just has not thought of. Sometimes this can make the experiment seem to work when it has not, as well as make it fail. One scientist conducted lots of demonstrations to show that a clever horse called Hans could count things and tap out the answer with his hoof. The horse was indeed clever, but, later, it was found that rather than counting, he was getting clues from tiny unconscious movements of the scientist's eyebrows.

This is why it is very important when conducting experiments to be as rigorous as you possibly can. The more casual you are, the more "eyebrow factors" you will let in. There will always be some things that you cannot control. But the more precise you are, the less these are likely to affect the outcome.

What went wrong?

However careful you are, your experiments may not work. If so, you should try to find out where you went wrong. Then repeat the experiment until you are absolutely sure you are doing everything right. Scientists learn as much, if not more, from experiments that go wrong as those that succeed. In 1929, Scottish scientist Alexander Fleming discovered the first antibiotic drug, penicillin, when he noticed that a bacteria culture he was growing for an experiment had gone moldy—and that the mold seemed to kill the bacteria. A poor scientist would probably have thrown the moldy culture away. A good scientist is one who looks for alternative explanations for unexpected results.

Glossary

atom: Every substance is made of invisibly tiny atoms, which are the smallest units of any chemical element. Each atom has a nucleus, around which minute electrons whirl.

boiling point: The boiling point is the highest temperature a liquid can reach. When a liquid is heated, the particles vibrate faster and faster. More and more break free, rising from the surface or forming bubbles within the liquid. As the liquid boils, it bubbles and steams furiously.

colloid: A colloid is a liquid in which particles too small to see with the naked eye are held suspended.

condensation: Condensation is the change from a gas to a liquid. As a gas cools down, its particles move slower and eventually clump together. The gas then forms drops of liquid. Water vapor from the air condenses on cold surfaces as air cools.

evaporation: Evaporation is the change from liquid to gas. When a liquid warms up some particles move fast enough to escape from its surface and turn into gas. This is how wet clothes dry out in the sunshine.

freezing point: Freezing point is the temperature at which a liquid turns solid as it cools. The freezing point of water is 32°F (0°C).

incompressible: Impossible to squeeze smaller.

ion: An ion is an atom that has gained or lost some of its electrons (see Atom). This makes it electrically charged.

melting point: Melting point is the temperature at which a solid turns liquid as it warms up. The melting point of ice is 32°F (0°C).

molecule: A molecule is the smallest bit of a substance that can exist by itself. A molecule is made up from one or more atoms. Each molecule of a substance has an identical combination of atoms. Water molecules are made from three atoms: one oxygen and two hydrogen.

particle: Particles are the tiny bits from which all matter is made—too small to be seen except under very powerful microscopes. The biggest particles are molecules, then come atoms and a host of smaller particles.

plasma: The fourth state of matter, created when a gas is subjected to immense heat or a huge electrical current. Atoms in a plasma are ionized (become ions).

saturation: Saturation means completely full. Air is saturated when it cannot take up any more water vapor. A solution is saturated when it cannot dissolve any more of the solute.

solute: The part of a solution that has dissolved in the liquid.

solution: A liquid in which a substance is dissolved.

solvent: A liquid able to dissolve substances.

suspension: A liquid in which fine specks of solid are mixed but not dissolved.

Index